IMAGES OF WAR WITHDRAWN
ADOLF HITLER

IMAGES OF WAR
ADOLF HITLER

NIGEL BLUNDELL

Pen & Sword
MILITARY

First published in Great Britain in 2017 by
PEN & SWORD MILITARY
an imprint of
Pen & Sword Books Ltd,
47 Church Street,
Barnsley,
South Yorkshire.
S70 2AS

A CIP record for this book is available from the British Library.

ISBN 978 1 52670 199 2

Typeset by Chic Media Ltd

Printed and bound by CPI Group (UK) Ltd, Croydon, CR0 4YY

Pen & Sword Books Ltd incorporates the Imprints of
Pen & Sword Aviation, Pen & Sword Maritime, Pen & Sword Military, Pen & Sword Family History, Pen & Sword Discovery, Wharncliffe Local History, Wharncliffe True Crime, Wharncliffe Transport, Pen & Sword Select, Pen & Sword Military Classics, Leo Cooper, The Praetorian Press, Remember When, Seaforth Publishing and Frontline Publishing.

For a complete list of Pen & Sword titles please contact
Pen & Sword Books Limited
47 Church Street, Barnsley, South Yorkshire, S70 2AS, England
E-mail: enquiries@pen-and-sword.co.uk
Website: www.pen-and-sword.co.uk

Introduction

There is usually something in a man's face that gives a hint as to his character. In the case of the young Adolf Hitler, however, there was no clue. No warning to the world.

The intriguing mystery about the rise of history's most despised despot is just how completely ordinary he once seemed. A chubby child, a mummy's boy, an idle student, an undistinguished artist, a disgruntled ex-soldier, a self-pitying social outcast, a face in the crowd… the early images of him give no indication of the demonic spirit that created this twentieth-century tyrant.

Only later in his tormented life came the metamorphosis, and it is fascinating to see how this mundane mask gradually fell away to reveal the manic monster lurking beneath.

The aim of this book is to trace this dramatic process in photographs – some iconic, some rare and intimate – of a man whose destructive legacy still touches us today.

These archive images cover the life of the seemingly unexceptional son of a minor customs official in provincial Austria as he rebuilt a German empire from the ashes of World War I defeat – and led it into a new dark age.

They demonstrate the spellbinding effect that Hitler had over his followers as he developed his oratory from his early beer hall meetings to his later mass rallies.

They reveal his mesmerising power over ordinary members of the public, both male and female, who readily accepted the myth of an Aryan race of young blond demigods – as propounded by a squat, dark-haired man with a comic moustache, poor health, chronic flatulence and, ultimately, opiate addiction.

Even more difficult to comprehend is the spell he cast over cynical diplomats, hard-headed business leaders and global opinion makers. The original captions to many of the contemporary photographs in this book are reverential in their descriptions of 'Herr Hitler, the German Chancellor', the person Time magazine proclaimed as its '1938 Man of the Year'.

Only months later, bent on global domination, he launched a war ultimately involving 61 countries and 1.7 billion people, three-quarters of the world's population. The death toll was more than 50 million.

The fascination with the cataclysmic events he caused remains as strong today as it did in the previous century. The mystery of how one man could exert so much power over so many people that he was able to plunge the whole world into war remains unanswered.

But the changing faces of Adolf Hitler, portrayed in this book from pampered baby to bar-room rabble-rouser to ranting megalomaniac, provide for us a graphic insight into the mind of a monster and the instigator of history's bloodiest drama.

The character of Adolf Hitler, as legend probably correctly has it, was built on the foundation of a harsh father and a doting mother. There is no reason to believe that the former, a stiff and formal civil servant, did not love his son. However, intensely proud of his rise to middle-class respectability, he demanded impeccable behaviour from his family, reinforced by violent punishments. Thus it was his mother whom the young Adolf revered. She gave him the affection that his father seemed unable to. In short, she loved her son too much. The result was that, ironically, the man who ended up a ranting tyrant spent his childhood as a bit of a 'mummy's boy'.

Adolf Hitler was born an Austrian citizen and a Roman Catholic at 6.30pm on 20 April 1889 at Braunau-am-Inn, close to the border with Bavaria. His mother, Klara, was the third wife of his father Alois, a customs official in the Austro-Hungarian Empire.

Contrary to the story that gained credence during the war, Hitler was not illegitimate. He did not carry his grandmother's name of Shicklgruber because, although his father Alois had been born out of wedlock, he subsequently had his birth legitimised by persuading the local priest to alter his birth documents to give him

Baby Adolf (above) was doted on and spoiled by his mother Klara. His father Alois, however, was a strict disciplinarian.

The birthplace of Adolf Hitler at Braunau-am-Inn, Austria, on 20 April 1889.

his father's name of Hitler. The confusion over Hitler senior's documents allowed later detractors to allege that Hitler's real maternal grandfather had in fact been a Jew named Frankenberger, who had been in the household where Alois's mother, Maria Anna Shicklgruber, was in service.

Yet there is no doubt that Alois Hitler's private life was less than orthodox. When his first wife died in 1883 he married his mistress, who was pregnant with their second child. When she too died shortly afterwards he married his second cousin Klara Polzl, who was 23 years his junior and also carrying his child.

Adolf was the fourth of six children. Two older brothers and a sister died in infancy and a younger brother died of measles at the age of 11, reportedly affecting young Adolf deeply. This meant that his only surviving sibling was a younger sister, Paula. From his father's second marriage, there was also a half-brother Alois, who ran away from home at the age of 14, and a half-sister Angela, later to become the housekeeper at Hitler's Bavarian retreat of Berchtesgaden.

Adolf's actual place of birth was a room on the first floor of a three-storey house, the ground floor of which was an inn called Gasthof Zum Pommer. His parents rented a suite of rooms above the hostelry where Alois reputedly drank to excess in the saloon downstairs before staggering upstairs to abuse his timid wife.

The family continued to live in Braunau-am-Inn until 1892 when they moved to Passau, where the River Inn joins the Danube. Only recently has it emerged from old newspaper cuttings that a four-year-old child, believed to be Adolf, was rescued from drowning in the river in 1894. In Passau, the Austrian customs house lay on the German side of the border, so Adolf, then aged three, grew up speaking German with a Bavarian accent, rather than the more cultured tones of a Viennese.

Ten-year-old Adolf, with arms folded, is centre of the top row in this photograph taken at his junior school in 1899.

Another school photograph, taken perhaps a year later (Adolf arrowed).

Adolf was educated locally at village and monastery schools, until the age of 11 when his father paid for him to attend secondary school, with the intention that he would also become a civil servant. But by then the years of his mother's mollycoddling – she had convinced herself that the boy was in poor health and needed constant attention – had made him a less than dedicated pupil.

At school he was a reasonably able pupil, although too shiftless to continue for long in any project. He failed exams and was refused promotion to the next grade. A teacher later recalled him as one who 'reacted with ill-concealed hostility to advice or reproof, at the same time demanding of his fellow pupils their unqualified subservience, fancying himself in the role of leader'. According to the myth later perpetuated by Nazi propagandists, Hitler the schoolboy led all the playground games, being a natural leader and 'understanding the meaning of history'. In reality, the young Adolf was a dreamer who made few friends.

On his retirement in 1895, Alois had moved his family to Leonding, near Austria's third largest city Linz, which Adolf thereafter considered his 'home town'. There, in 1903, his father walked to his favourite inn where he ordered a glass of wine but collapsed and died of a lung haemorrhage before it arrived.

Young Adolf, now 13, broke down and cried when he saw the body laid out. A local newspaper published an obituary that included the following telling description of the deceased: 'The harsh words that sometimes fell from his lips could not belie the warm heart that beat under the rough exterior.' But for Adolf, there would be no more harsh words and no more discipline from his domineering father, whose death had left the family with a healthy pension. The teenager abandoned all scholastic efforts to pursue his dream of becoming a great artist.

Thanks to his mother's generosity, he was able to live idly in and around Linz, where he was to be seen carefully dressed and sporting an ivory-tipped cane, attending the theatre or strolling the fashionable streets. Lacking any real occupation, he instead spent hours creating designs of a new and rebuilt Linz – youthful designs he was to turn to for comfort years later as Berlin was pounded to rubble in the final days of his life.

He bought a lottery ticket and dreamed of a future of artistic grace and leisure. When the number failed to come up, he denounced first the lottery organisation then the cheating government. He took piano lessons and then gave them up. Hitler succumbed to the grandiose music of Richard Wagner and was so stirred after a performance of his opera Rienzi that he walked with his sole boyhood friend, August Kubizek, and suddenly started to declaim about his future and that of his people. When he met Kubizek again 30 years later, he remarked: 'It began with that hour.'

When his mother died in 1907, Hitler moved permanently to Vienna where he had already unsuccessfully applied to enter the Academy of Fine Arts. Despite the knockback, the wayward dreamer found a dazzling new world opening up to him in the city, still at the turn of the century a faded hub of empire. In Vienna he discovered nationalism as a prime force in a multi-ethnic city humming with intrigue as the old Austro-Hungarian system started to break up. In particular, the ruling Germans had become a minority as the empire stretched into Czechoslovakia and the Balkans. Racism was rife, and since the mid-19th Century had focussed itself in particular on Jews, whose emancipation in Austria had for years been encouraging streams of immigrants from Hungary and the East. Between 1850 and 1910, their presence in Vienna had risen from two percent of the population to almost nine percent.

In Mein Kampf (My Struggle), Hitler's credo and political life story, he wrote of an orphaned youth of 17 'forced to go far from home to earn his bread'. The reality is very different. Having lived quite comfortably off his widowed mother for several years, he was able to continue receiving his father's state pension by fraudulently claiming to be in full-time education.

In 1908 Hitler was joined by his old friend Kubizek, who was studying music at the Vienna Conservatory. The two shared an apartment, but while Kubizek worked hard at his studies, Hitler seemed content to continue his aimless course. He made plans to tear down and rebuild the Hofburg, he sketched castles and theatres, he developed a recipe for a non-alcoholic drink, he composed pamphlets attacking landlords, he tried to write an opera and a drama. He painted but was rejected a second time when he tried to enter the Academy of Fine Arts. Its director advised him to try architecture, but here he failed because he had not passed his final exams at school, which were a prerequisite for entry.

A pencil-and-watercolour of the Karlskirche, Vienna, painted by Hitler at the age of 17. His work, though competent, failed to impress the city's Academy of Fine Arts.

Jealous of his friend Kubizek's relative success, Hitler abruptly left the shared apartment and rented a room by himself. Nearby was a shop that sold periodicals including one edited by a defrocked monk who called himself Jorg Lanz von Liebenfels. This magazine, Ostara, carried such headlines as: 'Are You Blond? Then You Are A Creator And Preserver Of Civilisation'. It invented a world of Teutonic blonds forever beset by mixed race, swarthy subhumans. It advocated castration and selective breeding and programmes of sterilisation, deportation of undesirables to an 'ape jungle' and liquidation by forced labour and murder. These themes were to play a large part in Hitler's later life.

In 1909 Adolf Hitler gave up his room and passed through several addresses, finally ending up sleeping on park benches until the winter forced him to seek shelter in a men's hostel. Here, among the derelicts, the habitual loner found one friend, a vagabond called Reinhold Hanisch. The pair teamed up and Hanisch managed to sell a number of Hitler's paintings. Finally, they quarrelled over a picture of the Vienna parliament building, which the artist felt was worth 50 crowns but which Hanisch had sold for only 10. In 1938, when he was in a position to do so,

A face in the crowd... The throng in Munich's Odeonplatz cheer Germany's declaration of war in August 1914. Years later Hitler befriended the photographer, Heinrich Hoffman, and mentioned that he had attended the event. Hoffman dug out the print and identified the future Führer.

Hitler titled this watercolour 'A Ravine near Ypres' where, in this small dugout at Wytschaete, Belgium, in 1914, he is credited with saving his commanding officer's life.

Hitler had his only friend from these miserable years tracked down and murdered.

By 1913 Hitler had despaired of finding the success that always seemed to elude him in Vienna. Partly for this reason, he moved on to Munich. More pressing, however, was his imminent call-up into the Austrian army. He was eventually arrested by the German police and sent home to report for his medical but was rejected by the Austro-Hungarian army as being 'too weak and unfit to bear arms' – although refusal on such grounds was not unusual given the state of the nation's health at the time. At this stage he had few political ideas but he had certainly acquired the current vogue of anti-Semitism, which had been around since the Pharaohs, was prevalent in Germany and Austria throughout Hitler's youth and which was to become the basis of his later credo.

On the outbreak of war, Hitler petitioned the Kaiser to allow him, although an Austrian, to join a German regiment. Within a week he had been enrolled in the 6th Bavarian Reserve Regiment, his medical problems evidently overlooked. In the army his life was to change. Here he finally found the discipline he may subconsciously have longed for. Though he remained a loner, he also found the equivalent of a family. At any rate, he was essentially happy and he served with distinction as a courier on the killing fields of Flanders.

Hitler painted this watercolour of a ruined cloister in Flanders in December 1917.

Hitler's baptism of fire was at Ypres and he was always prepared to take on dangerous missions. He won the Iron Cross (second class) that was later converted to first class – a rare honour for an enlisted man. The Iron Cross, awarded on the recommendation of the regiment's Jewish adjutant, stood him in good stead later when he needed to obtain acceptance as a German.

Army life also helped crystallise Hitler's political dogma. He said later that he thought of the war not in the same terms as other soldiers – getting through a battle unharmed and finding somewhere warm to sleep – but rather as a general or a politician, examining the grand scope of a military thrust and bewailing the 'enemy within'. These, in his eyes, were the pacifists, profiteers and Communists, whom he saw as more dangerous than the range of forces mobilised against Germany.

Grandly moustachioed Hitler is pictured (above) on the far left of his fellow soldiers of the 16th Bavarian Reserve Infantry Regiment. In a similar grouping he is seated to the right.

Hitler, wearing a 'pickelhaube' helmet, shares a dugout in 1916. Later that year he is shown (top row without a cap) recovering in a field hospital from a leg wound after being injured by shrapnel. In 1918 he was again hospitalised – more seriously after being nearly blinded in a gas attack.

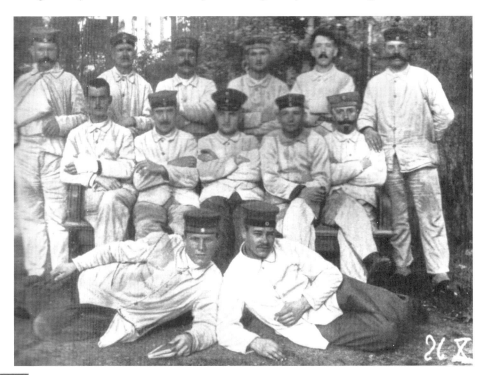

At the end of the war, Hitler was in hospital as a consequence of a British gas attack on his position. Defeat was a bitter pill to swallow, and for him now there could be only one reason for it: the Fatherland had been betrayed, not just by the Marxists and Jews, but also by the politicians.

Defeat brought terrible consequences to Germany. The Treaty of Versailles was imposed on a subjugated nation, under the terms of which the industrial half of Silesia and much of West Prussia was ceded to Poland, Schleswig-Holstein was ceded to Denmark, Malmedy was given to Belgium and Alsace-Lorraine to France. The Rhineland was demilitarised, the army was limited to 100,000 men and, even worse for the German psyche, insulting assumptions were made that Germany should admit sole guilt for the war and hand over certain officers to the victors as war criminals. In addition, harsh war reparations were demanded that left an impoverished Germany seemingly without hope. Not surprisingly, disaffection became widespread.

For the most part, this found its outlet in the spread of Communism, which had succeeded in overthrowing the established order in Russia. Following the 1917 October Revolution, Marxist ideology and egalitarian principles had been promulgated throughout the defeated nations with a great deal of success. The drift to Bolshevism, however, was not without its strident opposition. A strong sense of nationalism first found vent in the coffee houses and bourgeois clubs, where it was translated into political parties and groupings. Hitler, already noted by various right-wing army officers for his anti-Bolshevist views, became their semi-official mouthpiece, addressing and reporting on the nationalist groups.

In September 1919, Hitler now aged 30, found himself in the audience at a meeting of the German Workers' Party, a 40-strong group that purported to attack both business cartels and trade union tyranny. Its leader, Anton Drexler, declared the party to be a 'classless, socialist organisation, to be led only by German leaders'. National Socialism had begun. At the meeting, Hitler was inspired to get up and speak. His words impressed Drexler so much that he was invited to join the party's committee. It was while addressing a party meeting in this capacity two months later that he made the most significant discovery of his life. He had the gift of oratory. And he had what he had subconsciously craved ... an audience to whom he could present himself as a messiah.

Hitler discovered a gift for almost mesmeric public speaking. He threw himself into the organisation of the party, taking it over completely. He changed its name to the NSDAP, short for the *Nationalsozialistische Deutsche Arbeiterpartei* (National Socialist German Workers' Party) and developed a programme offering land reform, the abolition of ground rent and various other anti-capitalist notions. He also discovered the value of propaganda — the more half-baked the idea, the louder you have to shout it.

Copying a tactic from the Communists, he sent lorries packed with supporters around the streets. He dressed them in brown-shirted uniforms and his first public meeting in 1920 attracted 2,000 people. Soon his uniformed ex-army supporters were replaced by semi-terrorist thugs sporting his new party emblem, the swastika. Meanwhile, he consolidated his grip on the party. He acquired (probably with money secretly donated from army funds) the local newspaper, the *Münchener Beobachter,* and relaunched it as the *Völkischer Beobachter* (the People's Observer). As his fame spread outside Munich, important new allies were joining him.

Among these were his loyal deputy Rudolf Hess, Nazi philosopher Alfred Rosenberg, rabble-rousing Ernst Rohm and Julius Streicher, editor of the anti-Semitic publication *Der Sturmer.* However, the greatest triumph at the time was to sign up air ace Hermann Goering, the last commandant of Baron Von Richthofen's 'flying circus' and a national hero. All these disparate characters held extreme nationalistic views but they had one principal belief in common — a vitriolic hatred of the Jews.

After the war Hitler, the former itinerant artist, set about creating a new, smarter image for himself. These portraits from 1921 show his neatly parted hair had not yet been trained across his forehead.

In 1921 Hitler began to spread that message of hate in Berlin, where he found a ready group of listeners among those who were sickened by the decadence into which the capital had sunk. His ill-disciplined gang of thugs – that later were to become the highly-organised SA (*Sturm Abteilung,* or Storm Troopers) – were to be seen all over Bavaria beating up political opponents, ripping down rival election posters and openly collecting cash for the 'massacre of the Jews'. Any heckler who dared oppose a party speaker at a meeting was soon surrounded by these so-called brownshirts and severely beaten for his pains.

At last the government acted. When the SA disrupted a rival political meeting and assaulted its speaker, Hitler, now officially known in the party as the Führer, was sentenced to three months in jail. He served four weeks and was released a martyr and something of a folk hero. If the chaos after the war had been the launching pad for a fascist-style party ostensibly offering order, it was a twin stroke of fortune for Hitler that propelled the NSDAP into the forefront of national politics.

First, Germany could not pay the war reparations imposed by the Treaty of Versailles and, when she defaulted, France occupied the Ruhr, the heartland of German industry. This, in turn, contributed massively to the rampant inflation that spiralled out of control through the early 'Twenties, creating poverty and bitterness among the hitherto affluent middle classes.

Hitler and Rudolf Hess, leaning back behind him, relax on a break by horse-drawn carriage. When this photograph emerged in Britain, it was captioned as being from his private album and showing the future leader and his deputy staring across the coast towards England.

PERNET   Dr. WEBER   FRICK   KRIEBEL   LUDENDORFF   HITLER BRÜCKNER   RÖHM   WAGNER

Hitler poses alongside other conspirators in the 1923 Munich Beer Hall Putsch. Centre is the much-decorated General Erich Luddendorff and second from right is future SA leader Ernst Rohm.

A grim carload: Hitler and some of his close associates in 1923.

Hitler alongside his most high-profile and prestigious supporter mark 'Tag der Deutschen Einheit' (German Day) in October 1923, the month before the failed Munich Beer Hall Putsch, aimed at sparking a popular revolution.

Hitler the street orator strikes a pose before addressing a party rally in Nuremberg. The young girl on the right looks less than impressed.

Some of the first Nazis –
looking faintly ludicrous in
this proudly-signed souvenir
showing four thugs in boots
and their leader in shorts.

Hitler and his henchmen at
the party's Nuremberg Rally
in September 1923. It was a
modest affair compared
with the stage-managed
extravaganzas that would
follow in the 'Thirties.

In 1923 Hitler launched what was to become known as the 'Beer Hall Putsch'. What is often forgotten is that this bid to spark what Hitler declared a 'national revolution' was attempted with the backing of his most high-profile ally, the World War One military supremo General Erich Ludendorff. The old soldier later fell out with the Nazis but in the early 'Twenties, standing alongside Hitler and his otherwise less-than-impressive supporters, he was crucial to the prestige of the party. With Ludendorff's backing, therefore, in November 1923 Hitler was able to persuade a packed meeting in Munich's Burgerbraukeller that the Bavarian government had been overthrown and set off with his private army to march on Berlin – just as the political messiah of fascism, Benito Mussolini ('Il Duce' to his followers), had marched on Rome. Hitler's 2,000 followers, however, got no further than the centre of Munich before they were broken up by the police, resulting in the deaths of 16 Nazis and four officers.

A serious pose from the man charged with treason after his failed attempt at revolution.

Well aware of the propaganda value of these images, Hitler poses in Landsberg Prison in 1924 to capitalise on his role as a 'martyr' to national socialism.

Although the charge was treason and he initially faced a six-year sentence, Hitler was treated as a celebrity in Landsberg Prison and given VIP treatment. Visitors including the faithful Rudolf Hess (above, second from right) were permitted to come and go as they pleased.

Pressure from his party supporters forced the authorities to free Hitler in 1924. The photograph of him leaving Landsberg was taken by his friend Heinrich Hoffmann. The jailbird had used his nine months of cushy incarceration to write the first part of his political manifesto *Mein Kampf* (My Struggle). The initial volume was published the following year and the second volume in 1926.

Arrested two days later, Hitler was tried for treason and found himself facing a six-year jail term. In Landsberg Prison, he was treated like a celebrity and he used his time there to write *Mein Kampf*, his doctrine and vision for an imperial Germany (the 'Thousand Year Reich'), most of which was dictated to his faithful deputy and fellow prisoner Rudolph Hess. Hitler served only nine months but, by publicising his plight, made the most of his role as 'martyr' to the cause of national socialism. The most important lesson he learned from his incarceration was that the path to power lay not through brute force but by seemingly legitimate means.

Following his release from Landsberg Prison, having learned the lesson that his path to power need not be forged by brute force, Hitler reorganised the Nazi party to consolidate his position at its head. He also used his mesmeric oratory and the power of the camera to create the image of a natural leader of the German nation.

A rare photograph of Hitler in an SA cap, taken by Heinrich Hoffman.

When he was released in 1924, Germany's fortunes had changed again. The French were withdrawing from the Ruhr, inflation was being pegged and the NSDAP had been routed at the polls. A new approach was needed and Hitler rose to the challenge. He became a born-again democrat but at the same time strengthened and reorganised the SA, under the leadership of its co-founder, the scar-faced ex-army officer Ernst Julius Gunther, whose real loyalty was still with the regular army. Partly because of this, Hitler created his own bodyguard, the SS (*Schutz Staffeln* or Protection Squads), which were to be mobilised so effectively when in 1929 they came under the control of the sinister Heinrich Himmler.

At the same time, a revolt by certain NSDAP branches, who wanted to return to the socialist aspects of National Socialism, was quelled so successfully by Hitler that one of the leaders, a club-footed failed novelist called Joseph Goebbels, came

By 1927, the Nazis' annual Nuremberg rallies became ever more grandiose – and a political publicity coup for the party's leader.

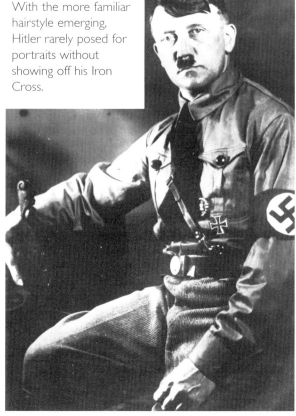

With the more familiar hairstyle emerging, Hitler rarely posed for portraits without showing off his Iron Cross.

At Nuremberg in 1929 Hitler grasps the so-called 'Blood Flag', supposedly stained by one of the Nazis who fell in the Munich putsch.

over completely to the Führer and was sent as gauleiter to clean up the particularly mutinous Berlin branch of the party. It was the start of the march to power.

Hitler was, by 1928, a national figure. Though still not taken seriously by the traditional parties, nevertheless the Nazis had polled 2.6 percent of the vote and a dozen deputies, including Goebbels, took their seats in the Reichstag. The tide finally turned with the collapse of the New York stock exchange when the rigours of depression hit the world. As Germany's dole queues lengthened to six million, agitators stirred up unrest. The nation's misfortune was blamed, as ever, on the Jews. Party membership spiralled. After the elections of 1930 the Nazis had 107 deputies, second only to the Social Democrats with 143 and well ahead of the Communists' 77. The nation had become ungovernable democratically and for several years the Weimar Republic president, war hero Field Marshal von Hindenburg, ruled by decree.

In 1932 Hitler stood against Hindenburg in a presidential election. Mass meetings, torchlight rallies and, for the first time, use of aircraft to carry the Führer to meetings the length and breadth of Germany attested to the genius of propaganda chief Goebbels. Hitler lost to Hindenburg — but he had won 37 percent of the vote. This support was translated into seats when elections were called later that year. Hitler's Nazis became the biggest single party in the Reichstag, with 230 deputies. Though they had not got a majority, power seemed a heartbeat away. Hitler, however, refused to deal with the Social Democrats. He was prepared to wait.

Hitler was relying on 'people power' to impel him to ultimate dictatorship. The level of hysterical adulation for him was fuelled by Goebbels' propaganda machine and can be gauged by a contemporary book that, although an official Nazi party publication, would now be considered little more than a 'fanzine'. *Deutschland Erwache* (Germany Awaken) is filled with dizzy words of hero worship and ludicrous 'pin-up' pictures that to modern eyes make the Führer seem more like a twerp than a tyrant.

In December 1931 Hitler acted as witness to the marriage of Josef Goebbels and previously-wed divorcee Magda. Ironically, it is likely that her father was a Jewish businessman, subsequently divorced and disavowed by her mother.

Like most politicians before and since, Hitler realised that being photographed with children – hugging them, patting their cheeks – would create an image of a caring, compassionate, family-loving leader of his people.

Even when issued to the British Press, such photos were captioned in adulatory terms, such as: 'These interesting photographs reveal an intimate and human side of his personality of which hitherto little has been heard. They show him in private life, on familiar terms with friends and neighbours, with children and with animals.'

Hitler enjoyed relaxing outdoors – and the photos of him doing so were not purely PR. The image of him sitting on a picnic rug while peeling an apple was taken by Heinrich Hoffman. The less professionally shot photograph of a group picnic required heavy retouching when published in the British Press. The original caption, as filed from Germany, translates as: 'He adores the simple life in the open'.

Man in the news. By the early 'Thirties, the former street-fighter was able to read about his political successes rather than his rabble-rousing.

In his mountain retreat. In 1933, with funds from the sale of *Mein Kampf*, Hitler bought a chalet near Berchtesgaden in the Bavarian Alps. Vastly expanded over the next two years, it was renamed The Berghof and became his favourite haunt.

The author gushes: 'We who have had the privilege of being able to work with him have come to worship and love him.' He describes the mass-murdering monster as 'honest, steadfast and modest', displaying 'strength and kindness'. His 'grandeur and deepest humanity takes the breath away from those that meet him for the first time'. And even more euphorically: 'The roots of our world rest within him and his soul brushed against the stars and he nevertheless remained one of us.'

The author of this drivel was Baldur von Schirach, one of Hitler's earliest henchmen, whose long-forgotten book of hero worship was recently translated and reproduced by military history experts at Pen & Sword Books (republished in the Images of War series under the title The Rise of Hitler). Editor Ron Wilkinson explains its significance: 'It's a fascinating piece of history, showing exactly how the Nazi propaganda machine worked on impressionable young minds. These were the words and images they were being drip-fed all the time. Most people have since wondered how an entire nation could have been taken in by such an awful outfit as the National Socialist Party. This sycophantic document of the day gives us a clue as to how even an extraordinarily wicked person can be made to look saintly.'

Hitler so trusted his friend and personal photographer Hoffman that he allowed the issue of a series of snapshots showing himself in a more relaxed mood than his usual public image. In retrospect, they were more laughable than laudable.

This 'pin-up' picture of Hitler in shorts trousers was widely circulated – before being withdrawn on the subject's orders when he correctly decided that it was 'undignified'.

Among the most laughable photographs in the book are those of Hitler posing in short pants. Obviously stumped for words, von Schirach wrote simply: '*In der Kurz'n*' (In the Shorts). Hitler later decided that such images were undignified and prevented further publication of them. Other staged snapshots show Hitler meeting his adoring public. According to the captions, his staff love him: 'How their eyes light up when the Führer is close to them!' The workers love him: 'The son of the people. Nobody in Germany was so loved by the German worker. This love breaks out of them spontaneously when they see him. They all look on him as their rescuer and thank him with shining eyes.' Sinisterly, this being a book aimed at youngsters: 'The youth love him. Children try to get close to him everywhere so that they can give him flowers.' And, of course, his dogs love him: 'The Führer has a breed of the most beautiful Alsatians in his house in the mountains. He loves them almost as much as they do him.'

There were some who genuinely loved him, of course, and that brings us to the enigma of Hitler's sex appeal. If he was spellbinding at his early political meetings and at his later, stage-managed mass rallies, he was particularly so to the opposite sex. Indeed he often stated that these mass audiences were his only 'bride'. Why this was so is difficult to discern, possessing as he did a graceless gaucherie that left him stiff and formal at any gathering where people he instinctively recognised as his social superiors were present. Nonetheless, in the early years the fledgeling Nazi party gained much of its influence through women, who were perhaps initially overcome by his oratory. Many gave, or willed, large sums to the party. Middle-class hostesses, who felt particularly threatened by Communism, vied to have Hitler at their soirées.

Little is known, however, about Adolf's sex life. He had an early passion as a youth in Linz for a girl whom he saw regularly but never once spoke to. His first real relationship is believed to have been with Geli Raubal, the 17-year-old daughter of his half-sister Angela, who had come to keep house for Hitler in Munich in 1924. His relationship with his niece matured when her mother was moved to Berchtesgaden to become the housekeeper at his mountain retreat, the Berghof. Hitler and Geli, living alone at Hitler's fashionable Munich house, became inseparable. Over the years, however, he became utterly possessive and controlling and forbade her to socialise when not in his presence.

His first love... Geli Raubal was 17-year-old daughter of Hitler's Berlin housekeeper, his half-sister Angela.

It is not established beyond doubt that his relationship with Geli was even a sexual one. A friend, Kurt Ludecke, said: 'The special quality of Hitler's affection for her is still a mystery to those closest to him.' What is not in doubt, however, is that he was devastated when she died in September 1931. Geli's lifeless body was found in Hitler's apartment, shot by a bullet from his revolver. Hitler went into a profound depression that lasted for months. During the days after the funeral, Gregor Strasser, one of the party's earliest leading lights, remained with him for fear that he would also commit suicide.

The coroner's verdict was suicide but there were predictable rumours that it was Hitler himself who had pulled the trigger. Others speculated that she was pregnant by him and he had ordered her death. And there were theories that she made this final gesture to escape Hitler's perverted demands on her. A more likely catalyst, however, was the arrival on the scene of Eva Braun.

Hitler met Eva in October 1929 in the Munich photographic studio of Heinrich

Hoffman, whose wife had been one of the first society ladies to take Hitler under her wing, earning herself the title of *Hitler-Mutti* (Hitler's mum). Eva, then aged 17, working in Hoffman's shop and helping out in his studio, was an attractive, simple-hearted girl whose principal interests were the theatre, fashion and society gossip. She and Hitler are believed to have shared a platonic friendship for three years and became lovers only in 1932, a few months after tragic Geli's death, by which time Eva was aged 20.

Eva was not particularly well treated by her powerful but controlling lover, who initially maintained her in relatively mean circumstances and forbade her to smoke or even to dance or sunbathe. In her diary, she once noted that she was kept waiting for three hours while Hitler fawned over actress Annie Ondra, buying her flowers and inviting her to dinner. She also commented that Hitler had other affairs, noting sadly that 'he was fond of such dimensions'. Eva made two attempts at suicide. In 1932 she shot herself in the neck. A further attempt followed in May 1935, during a period of three months in which Hitler 'said not a kind word' to her.

His soul-mate... Like Geli Raubal, Eva Braun was just 17 when she met Hitler in Heinrich Hoffman's studio. This was a picture that Hitler supposedly kept in his wallet.

Only in 1936, when she replaced Angela Raubal as the housekeeper at Berchtesgaden, would the tension relax. Even then, Eva's closeness to the Führer was kept hidden. She was hardly ever allowed to show herself in Berlin and was sent to her room whenever guests arrived often having to use side entrances and back stairs. One humiliation came when Hitler told his favourite architect, Albert Speer, in Eva's presence that 'a man of intelligence should take a primitive and stupid woman'.

Eventually, Eva Braun would become an accepted member of Hitler's intimate circle, staying loyally with him until his ultimate destruction. In the 'Thirties, however, her role as Hitler's partner was kept from the German public. It did not fit the image of a leader dedicated only to the resurrection of his country and the wellbeing of its people.

The influence of such propaganda and the undeniable power of Hitler's oratory had its desired effect in 1933, the year of publication of *Deutschland Erwache* (Germany Awaken) – and the year that Germany failed to awaken to the unfolding nightmare of Nazi rule. For the call that Hitler had awaited came in January 1933 when he was finally made Reich Chancellor.

A salute from on high... Germany's new leader acknowledges the cheering crowds from his Berlin Chancellery office.

Hitler criss-crossed Germany by car and plane on exhausting but successful 'meet the public' tours.

At a reception in his honour at the capital's City Hall, Hitler enters his name in the so-called 'Golden Book of Berlin'.

The Chancellor delivers a speech of thanks to his SS troops and SA thugs for their 'discipline' during an anti-Jewish boycott in Berlin the previous day.

Inside the Buergerbraukeller, the Munich beer cellar where the early Nazis once met. The occasion is the tenth anniversary of the attempted putsch – and, being November 1933, it is the first anniversary since the party came to power.

A bronze bust of the new Chancellor is unveiled at the Kaiserdamm Hall in Berlin.

When off the podium and out of the public eye, Hitler could be at ease, particularly with the SS-Begleitkommando who constantly guarded him. Here he shakes hands with his favourite, Bruno Gesche, who rose to be Hitler's closest bodyguard and whose boss repaid his loyalty by never abandoning him, despite several drunken indiscretions.

Hardly a flattering portrait of Bruno Gesch, Hitler's favourite bodyguard.

Winter watch... Hitler with early members of his personal bodyguard unit, the SS Begleitkommando: Bruno Gesche (on Hitler's immediate left), Erich Kempka (on Hitler's immediate right), Adolf Dirr, August Koerber, Franz Schaedle. Below Hitler informally reviews his bare-headed guard.

Even then, he was not considered a serious threat. The older politicians thought they could control him and must have been increasingly alarmed as he gradually brought every aspect of government under his or his supporters' control. His intentions became clearer when he took measures against his opponents. Already comprehensive, he had the excuse to make them draconian when the Reichstag was burned down in February. He blamed the Communists and used the event as an excuse to attack them.

First he enhanced his parliamentary muscle by proscribing Communism and preventing the party's deputies from taking office. Civil rights were suspended, the process of weeding out the Jews from the professions began and an Enabling Bill was passed giving Hitler virtually unlimited power. The 'virtually' was removed from the equation with the death of Hindenburg in 1934. Hitler combined the roles of President and Kanzler (Chancellor). He was now unstoppable. He began huge rearmament programmes and even concluded a treaty with Britain that allowed him to increase the size of the navy.

By this stage, Hitler had adopted his 'trademark' hairstyle, slicked down across his forehead.

The eleventh anniversary of the Munich putsch being celebrated in 1934. The 2,000-plus veterans of the failed coup assembled in the Burgerbraukeller where Hitler had issued the dramatic but premature proclamation of the 'new Reich'.

A high-spirited Hitler has a reunion in Berlin with an old wartime comrade, Ignaz Westenkirchner, who had just returned with his family from the United States to support the new regime.

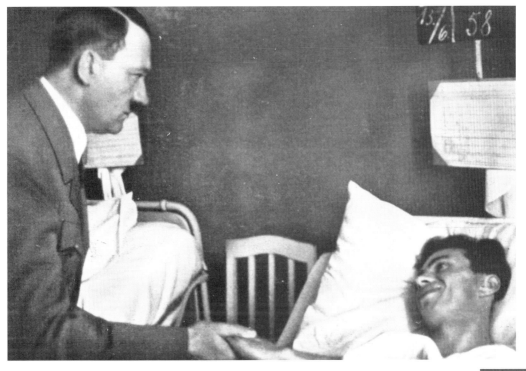

Visiting the sick: Hitler drops in on a ward at Reinsdorf Hospital, Lower Saxony.

Finger-wagging and posturing... Hitler had perfected his stage-managed style of oratory.

Upon becoming Chancellor, Hitler had appointed Hermann Goering as Prussian Minister of the Interior, in which position he headed the feared plain-clothes enforcers, the Gestapo, which he used effectively to silence his master's political opponents.

Riding in a Mercedes open-tourer, Hitler revisits Landsberg Prison, where he spent nine months in detention working on *Mein Kampf*, which he dictated to his fellow inmate and future deputy leader Rudolf Hess. One of his first acts on leaving the jail in December 1924 was to buy a supercharged Mercedes.

The Treaty of Versailles was torn up, conscription went ahead, books were burned, the first concentration camps were opened and a campaign of terror was launched by Nazi street gangs against political opponents and the Jews – an outpouring of hatred that ended in the infamous Kristallnacht (the Night of Broken Glass) when Jewish shops, offices and synagogues were attacked and glass littered the streets of every town. When Hitler suspected his old ally Rohm and the SA of plotting a 'second revolution' to oust him, he struck against them on the 'Night of the Long Knives'. In the purge, Rohm himself was dragged from bed (allegedly his young boyfriend's bed) and executed. Also executed that night was prominent politician Gregor Strasser who, although building the party from its earliest days, was now seen as a threat.

A visit to the theatre to see the 1935 premier of his favourite film-maker Leni Riefenstahl's propaganda movie 'Our Defence Force'.

Back to the Burgerbraukeller... Hitler greets a portly old comrade of his early struggle at a reception in Munich.

Women flocked to Hitler's side but this reception was something special. His favourite film stars make up the glamorous line-up: Else Elster and Leni Marenbach on his right and on his left English actress Lilian Harvey, Karin Hardt and Dinah Grace.

A visit to the Bavarian highlands to watch the winter sports meeting of the Nazi 'Strength Through Joy' movement in December 1935.

The opening of the 1935 Nuremberg rally... (from left) SS leader Heinrich Himmler, SA leader Viktor Lutze, Hitler, his deputy Rudolf Hess and Jew-baiting gauleiter Julius Streicher.

Guarding the Führer – not only from his enemies but from his supporters – became increasingly challenging, as cheering crowds greeted him whenever he stopped. As head of government, Hitler could call on all the security apparatus and police forces of the Weimar Republic but, as party leader, he continued to rely for personal security on an eight-man team plucked from the ranks of the SS and known as the *Begleit-Kommando*. Guarding the Führer in shifts 24 hours a day, they took no chances; they carried two pistols each and had 14 sub-machine guns between them with 2,500 rounds of ammunition. Hitler's unlikely favourite among them was Bruno Gesche, an ugly, cross-eyed street-fighting drunkard, whose boozy lapses in discipline were forgiven by his teetotal boss, who more than once rescued him from demotion and disgrace.

Hitler votes in the 29 March 1936 general election... Unsurprisingly, he cast the vote for himself – and indeed there was no opposition party for anyone to vote for!

Addressing members of his cabinet in the Chancellery while awaiting general election results in March 1936. The Nazis polled 99 per cent of the vote.

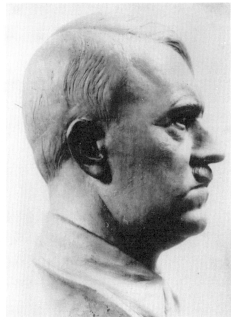

One of the many bronze busts of the Führer created at the time. This one, by sculptor Joseph Lymburg, was displayed in Leipzig's 'Hall of Honour'.

Picnic with a grand view... The Führer taking tea at his country estate, Berchtesgaden, perched 600 metres up the side of a mountain.

Hitler inspects a guard of honour outside the Reichstag in March 1936.

Receiving a handwritten copy on parchment of *Mein Kampf*. It took a year to transcribe.

The Nazi Party Congress opened in Nuremberg in September 1936. To Hitler's left are Julius Streicher and Rudolf Hess.

An iconic image of the Führer addressing a parade of 60,000 Hitler Youths and Girls at the Nazi Congress at Nuremberg on 12 September 1936.

An annual event: The sixteenth anniversary of the founding of the Nazi Party is held in Munich.

Hitler reads about the latest developments in German-Austrian relations while travelling on his special train.

Another flying visit, another child to greet him, another pat on the cheek: this time at the Berlin motor show.

A lakeside meeting with his ambassador to the United Kingdom, Joachim von Ribbentrop, whose expertise he came to rely on in his attempts to bamboozle the British into believing that Germany's intentions were peaceable. In 1938 he was promoted to foreign minister.

A friendly phone call from his study.

Discussing world affairs on the terrace at Berchtesgaden. Von Ribbentrop is seated on the far right.

Teenagers are invited to visit the Chancellery in Berlin. They are members of the Union of German Girls who are bound for the countryside where they are to spend a compulsory year of fresh air and outdoor activities.

The SS itself, which was only 280 men strong when Himmler had first taken control of it in 1929, had swiftly grown to more than 10,000. From these black-clad ranks, the Chancellor ordered the recruitment in March 1933 of a palace guard which became known as the *Leibstandarte-SS*. Staffed mainly ex-policemen, the RSD looked down on the likes of Gesche and his comrades in Hitler's escort group, viewing them (not unfairly) as brutish thugs untrained in detection techniques. Hitler was no intellectual snob and preferred to keep familiar faces close to him – old bodyguards such as Bruno Gosche.

All power was now in the hands of the Führer and his henchmen. In March 1936, in his first test of the world's resolve, he boldly marched 22,000 troops into the demilitarised zone of the Rhineland in direct contravention of the Treaty of Versailles. The world did nothing. Indeed, the world came to him as, on 1 August 1936, Hitler welcomed 3,963 athletes from 49 countries to Berlin for the 11th Summer Olympic Games.

It was ironic that the host of an event extolling the physical accomplishments of the human body was hosted by a man who was fast becoming a physical wreck. Indeed, it is utterly incredible to modern eyes how ordinary members of the German public, both male and female, readily accepted the myth of an Aryan race of young blond demigods as propounded by a squat, dark-haired man with a comic moustache, chronic flatulence and, ultimately, opiate addiction.

The Führer did become a comic character outside his homeland, of course, lampooned in cartoons and songs, particularly in Great Britain. One aspect of his imperfect physiognomy became an odd cameo of history – bawdy but worth repeating here because it reflects how a tyrant who would shortly have much of Europe quivering in terror could nevertheless become so dismissively viewed by the unbowed British. We are, of course, referring to a soldiers' marching song which alleges, in its opening line, that 'Hitler has only got one ball'. Where the rumour came from is unknown but evidence emerged many decades later that those singing it were not (with apologies for maintaining the vernacular) talking total b****cks.

The apparent proof that he had an undescended testicle comes from a medical examination of him in Landsberg prison in 1923 after his failed attempt to take power in the Munich beer hall putsch. Notes from Dr Josef Steiner described 'Adolf Hitler, artist, recently writer' as being 'healthy and strong' but suffering from 'right-side cryptorchidism'. This is when a testicle fails to descend from inside the body into the scrotum, as it normally does during childhood. The notes, held by the Bavarian government, were studied in 2015 by Professor Peter Fleischmann, of Erlangen-Nuremberg University, who took them as proof of one of Hitler's testicles being, as he put it, 'probably stunted'.

The records appear to go against a long-held theory that Hitler lost a testicle after suffering shrapnel wounds in the Battle of the Somme in World War One. That story had been given some credence in 2008 when a field medic's account emerged suggesting he had seen evidence of just such an injury. The medic, Johan Jambor, when interviewed in the 1960s, said he blamed himself for having saved the life of the future despot after finding him screaming for help. He added: 'His abdomen and legs were all in blood. Hitler was injured in the abdomen and lost one testicle. His first question was, Will I be able to have children?'

Some historians have disputed these claims, noting that Hitler's personal physician

Dr Theodor Morrell never mentioned the deformity in his private medical notes. Also, his family's original doctor Eduard Bloch reportedly told US interrogators that the Führer's genitals were 'completely normal'. Nevertheless, the soldiers' song, possibly written during the war by a British Council publicist to mock the Nazi leader and his cronies, caught on among servicemen and civilians alike and endured long after the war. For the sake of historical record, the satirical ditty, to the tune of the Colonel Bogey March, went: 'Hitler has only got one ball. Goering has two but very small. Himmler has something similar. But poor old Goebbels has no balls at all.' (Although it must be added there is no evidence Hitler's three henchmen had the testicular characteristics attributed to them!)

Even if the story of Führer's physical imperfection was true, it could have damaged only his pride, since it was far less serious a flaw than his host of other ailments. Medical evidence that came to light long after the war revealed that even by 1936 Hitler's health was so poor that he could barely function. He suffered from chronic bloating and took massive amounts of anti-flatulence drugs that contained small amounts of the nerve agent strychnine, an ingredient of rat poison. Hitler also had terribly bad breath, abscesses and gum disease. Other findings show that he had a mortal fear of cancer, suffered high blood pressure, cramps, headaches and had polyps removed from his vocal chords several times. He had eczema on both legs, so that he had to walk with bandages around his feet and could not wear boots. And because he had a fear of pills, most of the potions were administered by injection, say the 2013 study 'Was

The Führer's personal physician, Dr Theodor Morrell, who treated him with the most astonishing cocktails of drugs.

Hitler Ill?' written by historian Henrik Eberle and Hans-Joachim Neumann, a professor emeritus of medicine at Berlin's Charité University Hospital.

The man treating him was the aforementioned Dr Theodor Morrell, rumoured to be Jewish but who had managed to conceal the fact by joining the Nazi party and obtaining new identity papers. Morrell was regarded as a quack among many in the Nazi High Command and given the nickname 'Reich syringe master' by Luftwaffe chief Hermann Goering, himself a morphine addict by the war's end. For the Führer's eczema, Morell recommended the probiotic preparation Mutaflor. Hitler was cured and he appointed the doctor as his personal physician.

On 1 August 1936 Hitler opened the Summer Olympic Games in Berlin. For the first time a lone runner arrived bearing a torch carried by relay from the site of the ancient Greek games in Olympia.

Hitler welcomed 3,963 athletes from 49 countries to Berlin for the XIth Olympiad, designed as a mighty spectacle to show off Germany's power to the rest of the world and to reinforce the Nazi racial myth of a superior 'Aryan' civilization.

The Führer witnessed Germany emerging victorious from the XIth Olympiad, her athletes capturing the most medals. The organisation of the Games was also generally praised, the *New York Times* reporting that they had put Germany 'back in the fold of nations'.

Now, before every major speech, the Reich Chancellor allowed himself a 'power injection' in order to work at the peak of his capabilities. According to Norman Ohler, author of 'Blitzed: Drugs in Nazi Germany': 'Colds that could have kept him from appearing in public were banished by intravenous vitamin supplements. To be able to hold his arm up for as long as possible when doing the Nazi salute, Hitler trained with chest-expanders and also took glucose and vitamins. The glucose, administered intravenously, gave the brain a blast of energy after 20 seconds, while the combined vitamins allowed Hitler to address crowds wearing a thin uniform even on cold days without showing a sign of physical weakness.'

Girls from the German Singing Federation Festival in 1937 reach up to shake hands with their idol.

A young woman runs from the crowd at Thanksgiving 1937 to demand a dance from the Führer. Hitler seems happy to comply.

A greeting for a young woman in Bavarian costume at the National Agricultural Fair in Munich.

Italian Fascist leader Benito Mussolini pays a state visit and is driven in open car through the streets of Munich.

Hitler takes a break from talks with British Prime Minister Neville Chamberlain at a hotel in Bonn in September 1938.

The most controversial 'state visit' of all... The Duke and Duchess of Windsor are welcomed to Germany in 1937, much to embarrassment of Britain's new King George VI.

Hitler addresses an audience at Berlin's Sportspalast where for 90 minutes he ranted against the 'cruel' nature of the British Empire and threatened to overthrow it.

Hitler pays tribute at his parents' grave in Leonding, Austria, in March 1938 – a day before his triumphal drive to Vienna marking the 'Anschluss' (annexation) of his homeland.

The annual conventions of the Nazi Party were held every September between 1923 and 1938. They grew from a humble street gathering in Munich into the extravaganzas at Nuremberg in the late 'Thirties. They were propaganda spectaculars that both awed and frightened the world – and that was their aim.

From the podium... Hitler demands self-determination for the German minority of Czechoslovakians at Nuremberg.

Beneath the flag... Hitler peeks out from behind a swastika flag as he waits to speak at Nuremberg in August 1938.

The Führer speaks to the massed thousands. By 1938, up to one million people attended the rallies.

The Nuremberg rallies were not only parades of military might but displays of youth and health, aimed at proving 'Aryan superiority'.

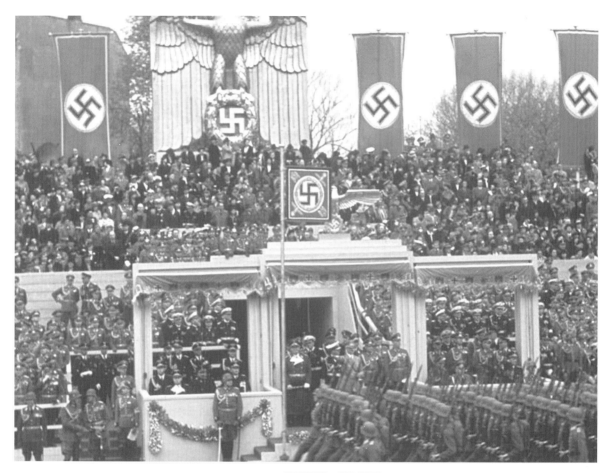

Nuremberg rallies were not the only example of the Nazis' genius for creating military spectacle. In the run-up to war, mind-bending fanatic Josef Goebbels, whose title was Minister of Propaganda and National Enlightenment, was granted an extravagant budget to orchestrate films, festivals, concerts, parades and march-pasts, like these in honour of the Führer.

Two faces of a tyrant... The messianic rantings of a madman at his rallies and the friendly aspect of a welcoming host entertaining a pretty guest. By the late Thirties, both facets of his character seemed to have deceived an entire nation.

Another year, another Putsch anniversary... Hitler addresses a memorial service for those killed in November 1923.

On a visit to Italy, Hitler is feted by Mussolini and shown some of the artworks of Rome. The two leaders and von Ribbentrop (far left) look slightly taken aback by the semi-nude statue.

Albert Speer shows his leader his grandiose plans for the reconstruction of the German capital.

On a visit to Austria, Hitler is cheered by the crowds as he enters the city of Linz.

Hitler enters Sudetenland at the head of his forces to the cheers of Germans living in that part of Czechoslovakia.

Hitler and his generals inspect barbed-wire defences on the Czech border that posed no barrier to the German army.

Planning a plebiscite to 'legitimise' Germany's annexation of Austria, Hitler and his hierarchy pose on the steps of Vienna's City Hall.

Hitler wearing spectacles at work in his Munich headquarters.

Continuing his tour to promote the Austrian plebiscite, Hitler entertains schoolgirls at an Innsbruck hotel.

Returning to Berlin, the Führer receives his customary euphoric welcome.

This, then, was the state of health of the man who – portraying himself as a vegetarian teetotaller who had long ago given up tobacco and who did not even touch coffee – welcomed the world's finest athletes to the 1936 Summer Olympics.

The German capital had been a popular choice of venue before Hitler came to power but in the run-up to the event protests grew. In the United States, Jewish groups, in particular, called for a boycott. They went ahead, however, and proved a massive propaganda coup for the Nazi regime. Much to the delight of Hitler and his swastika-waving spectators, the German team was the overall winner of the Games, with 32 golds, ahead of America's 24. The only embarrassment the Nazis suffered was that the undoubted hero of the Games was US athlete Jesse Owens, the grandson of slaves, whose medal-winning achievement made a mockery of the creed of Aryan superiority.

Show of force... On his fiftieth birthday, 20 April 1939, Hitler reviews a parade of troops, tanks and heavy-calibre guns.

Hitler poses with children as part of his fiftieth birthday celebrations.

A formal pose taken at Berchtesgaden – for once in an official photograph, he is shown wearing civilian clothes.

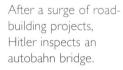

After a surge of road-building projects, Hitler inspects an autobahn bridge.

Time for celebration... Hitler entertains in style in his rebuilt Chancellery building.

The end of Czechoslovakia as an independent state... Hitler looks down from a hilltop on the city of Prague, which is now a supposedly German 'protectorate'.

Hitler, Hess and a secretary at Berchtesgaden.

Goering and Hitler discuss tactics during a train journey.

Flowers for the Führer from Hitler Youth members at a Berlin automotive exhibition.

Hitler in formal attire at a Berlin function.

Portrait of the Hitler in the window of a Prague restaurant in 1939.

Seemingly unaware of the camera, Hitler and Ribbentrop walk deep in conversation down a muddy track.

Hitler addresses the Reichstag in a speech rebutting a plea for peace by US President F.D. Roosevelt.

Bowing low: Poland's foreign minister Colonel Beck is greeted for 'friendly' talks at Berchtesgaden in early 1939. In September Germany invaded his country.

On 1 September 1939 Hitler declares war on Poland – and receives the ovation of the house. Behind him is the President of the Reichstag, Hermann Goering.

Flying over the Polish battlefields, Hitler observes the destruction of another independent nation – prompting the Allies to declare war on the Third Reich.

A view by periscope of the invasion of Poland. Hitler watches troop movements through the safety of a periscope.

Significantly, even as the Olympic Torch was being borne towards an Olympic stadium for the first time in a symbol of union between nations, German forces were on the march. The Condor Legion, a unit composed of members of the Luftwaffe and the Wehrmacht, were being sent to serve with the Nationalist army of General Francisco Franco in the Spanish Civil War. It was a bloody training exercise, particularly for the Luftwaffe, which got its first experience of bombing raids over Spanish cities.

There could be no further doubt about Hitler's intentions when, in March 1938, German troops marched into an acquiescent Austria. This *Anschluss*, or annexation, of Hitler's homeland was later accepted in a plebiscite by the Austrian people. The events of 1938 brought the biggest crisis to face Europe since World War I. Hitler clearly stated that his policy of *Lebensraum* would culminate in German possession of all lands inhabited by Germanic peoples. His next target was the Sudetenland, the part of Czechoslovakia that was inhabited largely by ethnic German speakers. After the Sudetenland, the rest of Czechoslovakia would undoubtedly follow. British Prime Minister Neville Chamberlain issued a warning that Britain would ally herself with France if Hitler proceeded along his desired course.

Hitler, however, dealt skilfully with the problem. At his Nuremberg Rally on September 12 he made his final demand for a peaceful ceding of the disputed territory and the next day the Sudeten Germans rose in an abortive revolt. Three days later Chamberlain flew to Munich and caved in to Hitler's demands. The Munich Agreement was signed by Germany, Italy, Britain and France; shamefully, Czechoslovakia was not consulted. Hitler sent the British leader home with a promise of 'peace in our time' on the infamous 'piece of paper' signed by Hitler.

With the Sudetenland ceded, Czechoslovakia's fate was sealed. In March 1939 German forces, including the SS and Gestapo, moved in and much of the rest of country was absorbed into the Third Reich. The invasion of Czechoslovakia spelled the end of the policy of appeasement. Hitler's word was shown to be worthless and the world awakened at last to his intentions. Britain and France pledged to support the independence of Hitler's next logical target, Poland.

Emboldened by his success and the weak European stance against him, Hitler in August 1939 signed a non-aggression pact with the newly emerged Soviet Union, itself founded only in 1922. This was more than just an alliance of convenience between two ideological enemies. For Russian leader Josef Stalin, it was the equivalent of Britain's Munich Agreement the year before. It bought him time. It also set out spheres of influence that would enable him to take his share of a partitioned Poland, should the Germans decide to invade. For Hitler, it meant one enemy fewer if Britain and France should make good their promises of coming to Poland's aid.

On 1 September 1939 Hitler marched into Poland ... and at last Britain and

France declared war. The Poles fought heroically, with horse-mounted cavalry charging German tanks, but the invaders managed to mop up Polish resistance within four weeks. With the connivance of Moscow, Hitler then partitioned the subjugated country and, safe in the east, he looked towards France.

Hitler had dreamed of an enlarged Europe dominated by Germans, with their racial brothers, the British, running their empire as a second power. For years he had been in contact with Nazi sympathisers in England and had been encouraged by the growth of Oswald Mosley's fascists. His cause was also bolstered by the seeming sympathies of the former King, Edward VIII, by now Duke of Windsor following his abdication. Even though his plans for a pact with Britain had come to nothing, Hitler still held the hope that it would fail to back up its pledges to Poland with armed action – and that France too would wish to avert another European war.

France's initial reaction was, to say the least, hesitant. On 7 September, in accordance with their alliance with Poland, French troops advanced from their defensive Maginot Line, the system of bunkers and forts along France's eastern border, and advanced a mere three miles into the German-occupied Saar region. There they met the Germans' thin and undermanned Siegfried Line and halted. And ten days later they withdrew back to their starting positions.

Following the Saar Offensive came a period of inaction that the British called the Phoney War, the French called Drôle de Guerre (joke war) and the Germans called *Sitzkrieg* (sitting war). During this period, Hitler still believed there was a chance that both France and Britain would make peace and on 6 October made a formal offer to both Western powers. Despite seeking peace with them, he was planning their destruction.

The non-aggression pact between Germany and the hated Soviet Union had gained Hitler the freedom to concentrate on his western neighbours. And whereas in September 1939 the French had mobilised 98 divisions with 2,500 tanks that theoretically could have overwhelmed the opposing German force of 43 divisions and no tanks, by the spring of 1940 the Wehrmacht had redressed the balance. Germany had mobilised more than four million soldiers, a million in the Luftwaffe and 180,000 in its navy and 100,000 in the *Waffen-SS*. Even allowing for the occupation of Poland – and for forces that had swept into Denmark and Norway – the German army had three million men, 2,439 tanks and 7,378 guns available for the offensive.

Prime Minister Chamberlain seemed unaware of this. On 2 April he announced that Hitler had 'missed the bus' in Europe. Britain's position was secure, he assured Parliament, in the wake of a string of trade agreements with Holland, Belgium and the Scandinavian countries. A month later Hitler began a full-scale invasion of those same countries…

This sequence of five photographs were taken when Hitler had only recently received word of France's capitulation. He appears to be almost dancing with joy at the news in June 1940.

The day after France signed the armistice with Germany, Hitler made a triumphal but fleeting tour of Paris on 23 June 1940. Accompanied by architect Albert Speer and his favourite sculptor Arno Breker, he spent just three hours in the city, visiting the Paris opera, the Champs-Elysees, the Arc de Triomphe and the Eiffel Tower.

On the evening of 10 May German forces occupied Luxembourg virtually unopposed. Overnight they moved into the Netherlands and Belgium. The French rushed across the Dutch border, only to find the Dutch already in full retreat. Along with the British Expeditionary Force, which had been sent to France at the onset of hostilities, the allies pushed their best forces into Belgium – but it soon became clear that by advancing into the Low Countries the Allies were dancing to Hitler's tune.

On 13 May, the allies were caught by surprise as a second German force emerged further south, through the Ardennes, near Sedan on the River Meuse. Panzers poured into France. The rout had begun and the race for the coast was on.

France folded as dramatically as it had before the Prussian blitzkrieg in 1870. The simple device of invading through Holland and Belgium had bypassed the mighty Maginot Line. The subsequent attack through the Ardennes had trapped the allies in a pincer movement, German tanks reaching the English Channel on 20 May.

The British attempt to shore up French resistance was ended with the heroic evacuation from Dunkirk. The losses of men and equipment on the Channel beaches in May and June might have been enough to revive talk of peace. Yet in Britain it was hailed as 'a deliverance' by Winston Churchill, who on 10 May had replaced the shamed Neville Chamberlain as Prime Minister. He was right. The vast majority of the British Army and the best of its equipment had been about to be swallowed up by the enemy. However, the men who flooded onto the beaches at Dunkirk received a valuable helping hand from Hitler, who instructed his forces to halt around the perimeter of the port.

This order still puzzles historians today. One explanation is that Hitler delayed a Panzer advance in order that the slower German infantry might catch up. Another is that Hermann Goering, the second most powerful man in the Reich, had persuaded Hitler to allow him, rather than the Wehrmacht generals, the glory of wiping the British army off the map. It was a disastrous decision for the Luftwaffe, which found itself hampered by cloud cover and RAF fighters. The result was that the Royal Navy, backed by an armada of little ships, plucked a staggering 338,000 British, French and Belgian soldiers off the beaches and returned them to English ports to fight again.

Meanwhile, the German forces turned south to Paris, opposed by the demoralised remnants of an army in total chaos. Nothing sums this up better than the situation at the vital canal crossing at Briare, in the Loire Valley, where there was only one telephone link between the French troops and their command – and that was out of action between midday and two o'clock while the postmistress had her lunch. Hitler ordered that the French surrender be signed at Compiegne in the same railway carriage in which Germany's capitulation to France had taken place in 1918.

The seemingly unstoppable Nazis had overwhelmed Poland, Norway, Denmark, Luxembourg, Holland, Belgium and France within the space of three months. And the victories were truly Hitler's, because only he had realised and acted upon the importance of tanks and heavy armour in modern warfare. Only he had conquered the problem of logistics and supply. Only he had made the trains run on time. Hitler had demanded long-range cannons on his tanks. He had equipped his Stuka dive-bombers with banshee, ear-splitting sirens. He had devised the plans for the sudden overthrow of his European neighbours. In due course, Hitler's judgment would once again fail. For now, however, he was the military genius of the age.

Even so, he read the signs wrongly. As he celebrated the defeat of France with a victory parade in Berlin in June 1940, when thousands of soldiers goose-stepped past their Führer, it was as if the war had been won. In fact, it was just starting...

By now, Hitler had a powerful though unpredictable ally in fascist leader Benito Mussolini of Italy. In 1939 the Germans and Italians had cemented their friendship with the so-called Pact of Steel, which committed both countries to support the other if one of them became involved in a war. Despite this, Mussolini declined to join Hitler in the invasion of Poland. But he did enter the conflict in 1940, fearing that Germany might otherwise get all the spoils of war. On 17 June, the date France sought surrender terms, Mussolini ordered his troops into southern France. A small area was occupied but the French put up fierce resistance and a full-scale invasion never occurred. Mussolini's other demands – of Corsica, Tunisia, Djibouti, Syria and Malta – angered the Führer, who told him bluntly that the time for such discussions would come only after Britain was out of the war.

When Winston Churchill took over as Prime Minister in London and inspired his countrymen with his defiance and determination to fight on, Hitler, alone among the Nazi leadership, realised that defeating Britain on continental Europe would not be the end of the British war effort. He knew the war would be continued from Canada or some other outpost of a worldwide empire. He could foresee that an English government in exile in Canada might certainly succeed in bringing the United States into the war, while the wholesale defeat of the British Empire would benefit no one but Japan and America.

For this reason, although Operation Sea Lion, his plan for the invasion of Britain, was launched, it was not Hitler's greatest priority. He still sought an alliance. Before he was prepared to attempt an invasion, he demanded 40 army divisions, a network of heavy artillery all along the French Channel coast and complete mastery of the air. And so began the Battle of Britain.

It was now the turn of the RAF to defend Britain's shores. Throughout the hopeless Battle of France, the RAF had lost almost half its strength. And in the summer of 1940, it faced the toughest challenge yet. First, the convoys supplying

Britain were the targets of the Luftwaffe. Then Fighter Command came under attack. The third phase turned the might of the German air force on to the civilian population of Britain. London and other major cities were bombed night after night. But most perilously, the airfields used by the defending fighter squadrons came close to being put out of action. Narrowly, however, the Spitfires and Hurricanes of the Royal Air Force, flown heroically by the gallant 'Few', defeated the German Luftwaffe. Britain, for the present, was safe.

Hitler turned again to siege tactics, throwing a ring of steel around the British Isles. By October 1940, Operation Sea Lion had been abandoned. Instead, submarines patrolled the seas to try to starve the enemy into submission. What Hitler needed more than military victory was a treaty with Britain to enable him to pursue his aims eastwards. He yearned to attack the despised Soviet Union but, with Britain still fighting on, there was always the danger of the USA joining the fray.

Which brings us to another unsolved mystery of World War Two: why did Hitler's second-in-command, Rudolf Hess, suddenly leave Germany and fly to Britain in 1941? Was Rudolf Hess's doomed mission actually approved by the Führer in advance in an attempt to bring the British into a war against the Soviet Union?

No one else in his entourage was as loyal to Hitler as Hess. He had marched with pistol drawn at the head of the group staging the infamous coup in 1923 and had later helped edit the manuscript of *Mein Kampf* at Landsberg Prison, where both men were held after the failed putsch. He had organised the SA stormtroopers in the party's early years. And it was Hess who, through intermediaries, had been responsible for maintaining links with pro-German circles in Britain.

Hess took off from an airfield near Augsburg, Bavaria, on the evening of 10 May 1941, a date chosen because an astrologist had told him the stars were in his favour. An expert flier, he piloted his Messerschmitt 110 for five hours until, reaching Scotland, he bailed out and allowed his aircraft to crash. He had been aiming to land near Dungavel Castle, South Lanarkshire, home of the Duke of Hamilton whom he had met during the 1936 Berlin Olympics.

Arrested by the Home Guard, Hess was taken the following morning to meet the Duke and told him he was on a 'mission of humanity' to bring the war with Britain to an end. When Churchill heard about the unexpected visitor from Germany, he refused any attempt at negotiation and instead had him brought to the capital – which had just seen 500 German bombers carry out their biggest attack yet – and locked him in the Tower of London. He remained in custody until, sentenced at the post-war Nuremberg Trials, he died in Berlin's Spandau Jail in 1987 at the age of 93.

Hess's flight to Britain has remained one of the great mysteries of World War II. Historians long assumed that Hitler's deputy was acting on his own. But in 2011 a

German historian researching the State Archives in Moscow uncovered a previously unpublished document that cast his notorious one-way trip in a new light. It was a handwritten report by Hess's adjutant Karlheinz Pintsch while a Soviet prisoner of war in 1948.

Pintsch had accompanied Hess to the airfield and the following day had delivered a letter to Hitler at The Berghof. According to eyewitnesses, the letter began with the words: 'My Führer, when you receive this letter I shall be in England.' According to the Pintsch account, Hitler 'calmly listened to my report and dismissed me without comment' – indicating that he had been well aware of Hess's flight.

Had Berlin been attempting negotiations with the British all along? Pintsch suggests so, writing that Hess's mission was 'by prior arrangement with the English' and that he had been authorised to 'use all means at his disposal to achieve, if not a German military alliance with England against Russia, at least the neutralisation of England'. So a peace offering to Great Britain made tactical sense at a time when it was the Wehrmacht's last fighting enemy and Hitler was preparing to attack the Soviet Union. It would have been very much in line with Hitler's stated policies to attempt to bring the British into a war against the Soviet Union.

Churchill's rejection of such a flawed olive branch did not deter the dictator from his plans for a campaign of eastward expansion just a month later. In the summer of 1941 Hitler emanated an aura of absolute power. Europe was at his feet. Fascism reigned supreme. Even Marshal Petain, leader of the collaborating French government based in Vichy, said: 'France had been morally corrupted by politics.' Democracy was in decline. Yet the decision to attack Russia before the war in the west had been won remains one of Hitler's least comprehensible decisions. There was a strategic logic to it, however.

With Britain under Churchill vowing there would be no peace with Germany, Hitler was becoming concerned with the gradually increasing role of the United States. It was the war he wanted to avoid. So it became urgent to defeat the only significant force left in Europe to face him: the Red Army. It was vital to remove this piece from the chessboard before any full-blooded intervention from across the Atlantic by the world's most powerful nation. At the same time, Stalin was increasing his strength. Hitler felt he had to strike quickly.

In his fantasies, he saw the rapid defeat of Russia as the final turning point. Not only would there be no European ally left for Britain, the Japanese would be freed from the giant at their rear to begin their southern expansion programme. This, in turn, would tie up America in the Pacific and force Britain to surrender. By sweeping through North Africa, Russia and the Near East, his way would be clear to Afghanistan, from whence he could strike at the jewel of Britain's empire, India.

It was the route to world domination. And it was within his grasp. After all, by the early summer of 1941 Hitler's forces had invaded and dismembered Poland, taken control of Norway and Denmark, crushed France and seen the British flee the Continent. They then conquered Yugoslavia, occupied Greece and removed the British from Crete. The Luftwaffe was pounding Malta. Britain's vital Atlantic supply line was being strangled by U-boats. In North Africa in the spring of 1941, the Nazis and their Italian allies swept through the deserts. Afrika Korps commander Generalfeldmarschall Erwin Rommel, the so-called 'Desert Fox', pushed the British back to Tobruk, tempted onwards by the glittering prize of the Middle-Eastern oilfields. Hitler's supposed ally, Russia, was also providing Germany with oil.

A massive empire was within sight if Hitler had allowed these operations to continue to fruition. Yet on 22 June 1941, despite cautionary advice from his generals, he began his own personal war. He launched Operation Barbarossa, with 153 divisions, 3,580 tanks and 2,740 planes against the Bolsheviks. He also launched a new terror: the notorious *Einsatzgruppen* (special squads) were unleashed with orders to exterminate Jews, gypsies, Asiatics, intellectuals, commissars or anyone capable of becoming a leader. The normal rules of warfare as practised in the west were suspended in Russia. The 'Final Solution', the annihilation of the Jews, had been extended to cover the Russians.

If the conquest of Russia had an element of logic in its conception, Hitler had ignored the lessons of Napoleon's disastrous campaign. He was aware of the huge empty spaces of the country and the fighting spirit of the Slavs. But he believed Moscow could be taken in six weeks – after which he planned to raze it and create a reservoir in its place.

That was his typically ambitious plan but also his biggest mistake, as analysed by leading military historian Andrew Roberts. In his book 'Storm of War', he argued that, instead of invading in 1941, Hitler should have concentrated on evicting Britain from Africa and the Middle East. As Rommel subsequently got to within 60 miles of the Egyptian border by October 1942 with only 12 divisions – a fraction of the three million men that Hitler threw against Russia – he could have swept the British out of Egypt and Palestine. Taking Cairo would have opened up the route to the virtually undefended oilfields of Iran and Iraq. It would also have expelled the Royal Navy from its Mediterranean base of Alexandria, closed the Suez Canal to Allied shipping and allowed an attack on British India.

Roberts says: 'Hitler could then have invaded Russia in his own time with his Army Group South moving only a few hundred miles from Iraq to Stalingrad, rather than more than 1,000 miles as it did in 1941 and 1942. A German invasion of the Caucasus and Southern Russia would have cut the USSR off from the main part of her non-Siberian oil supply and, as the German Panzer General Friedrich von Mellenthin noted, a motorised division without fuel is mere scrap iron.

'Considering how much Stalin decried the idea that Hitler would ever attack him in 1941 – despite no fewer than 80 intelligence reports from dozens of unrelated sources that Barbarossa was impending – there is no reason to suppose that the USSR would have been on any better war footing in the summer of 1942 or 1943 than it was in 1941.'

And yet, at first, things went Hitler's way. Victory at Kiev netted 650,000 prisoners. But the Russian 'scorched earth' policy of destroy and retreat was taking its toll. As the Russians melted away and drew the Wehrmacht ever deeper into the enormous, empty land, a typical German quip was: 'No enemy in front of us, no supplies behind us!'

Russian heroics and suffering at Stalingrad and elsewhere are now legendary. And at the gates of Moscow, Hitler came to the end of 20 years of unremitting success. By the autumn of 1942, the Russian campaign was going badly wrong. Stalin had decided the 'scorched earth' policy had gone far enough. There was now a massive German front exposed and seemingly endless supplies of Russian reservists were thrown into the fray.

Hitler's rages directed against his generals could not reverse the decline in the Wehrmacht's fortunes. By April, after a series of bitter battles, German casualties stood at more than a million, or over 31 per cent of his eastern army, which was stalled, tantalisingly, just sixty-two miles from Moscow.

The campaign was demoralising the Führer. Goebbels, visiting his master at headquarters, noted that he was 'very much aged ... serious and subdued'. Hitler began to complain that the sight of snow caused him physical pain. On a Bavarian mountain break in April, he was caught by a late snowfall. He hurriedly departed. 'It's a kind of flight from the snow', Goebbels wrote in his diary, making the link with the winter defeats in the east.

Even with the German advances in the late spring, Hitler's nerves were still unstable. And still he underestimated his opponents' capabilities. He gave the order to entrench in southern Russia, take the eastern oilfields and deny the Russians use of the agricultural lands. Once more his vision was betrayed by his army's incapacity. Even so, by 23 August, the Sixth Army had reached the Volga and Stalingrad.

The conquest of Stalingrad was meaningless in itself, as German troops already controlled the river traffic. Hitler, however, was a man with a mission. Despite the protests of the Chief of Staff, Field Marshal Franz Halder, that he could not sustain campaigns in both the Caucasus and Stalingrad, Hitler gave the order to attack. He fired Field Marshal Wilhelm List when the Caucasus campaign faltered and took command of Army Group A himself. Casualties continued to mount in the house-to-house battle for Stalingrad. His commanders begged him to halt the suicidal attacks. He ignored them. The city had become a matter of prestige.

Visit to an arms factory where their leader praises workers' role in the war effort.

Hitler with German and Italian generals on a visit to the Russian Front.

Examining war charts on the Russian Front are (from left) Italian General Ugo Cavallero, Mussolini, General Wilhelm Keitel, Hitler, General Alfred Jodl and a Major Christian.

Astonishingly, the German forces at the gates of Stalingrad and elsewhere were reliant not only on arms and ammunition to keep them going but on drugs – the use of which was by now endemic not only in Hitler's household but throughout the entire military machine and, indeed, much of the civilian population…

The extent of drug taking was revealed 70 years after the war by German historian Norman Ohler, whose research of military archives in his homeland and the United States changed perceptions of the Nazis' wartime successes. In his book *Der Totale Rausch* (Total Rush), Ohler says the Nazis had rejected recreational drugs such as cocaine, opium and morphine, which were readily available in Germany during the 1930s, condemning them as 'Jewish' opiates. The Third Reich's scientists were encouraged to find an alternative stimulant more suited to an Aryan master-race, and chemist Fritz Hauschild came up with a powerful methamphetamine-based alternative.

Manufactured from 1937 under the brand name of Pervitin, it was marketed as a pick-me-up pill designed to combat stress and tiredness and create feelings of euphoria. The Nazis wanted Pervitin to rival Coca-Cola, explains Ohler, so people took it, worked hard and were happy. To ensure that millions of German housewives were not left out, the Nazis even developed chocolates containing the drug.

The drug was freely distributed among the armed forces, which meant that Hitler's armies carried out their blitzkrieg invasions while high on a version of crystal meth, which kept them wide awake and feeling invincible. Initially, the army did not realise Pervitin was a mind-altering drug; soldiers thought it was just like drinking coffee. But the Nazi leadership was well aware of its value as a stimulant during combat. Having tested it in 1939 during the invasion of Poland, the army subsequently ordered 35 million tablets of Pervitin for soldiers before advancing on France in the spring of 1940.

Was Pervitin the real reason for the German army's initial successes? After all, in four days, Hitler's tanks captured more French territory than German troops had managed to secure in four years of the First World War. Pervitin helped the invading Nazis stay awake, keep going and, apparently, feel great. And drug-taking was not only used by the lower ranks. Erwin Rommel, who was decorated by Hitler as a tank commander during the invasion of France, is said to have consumed Pervitin 'as if it was his daily bread'.

However, as the Third Reich's theatres of war spread, even Pervitin could not conceal the fact that all was not going well for the Nazi conquerors. Hitler had become so immersed in his 'crusade' in Russia that he had neglected other fronts. The state of his physical and mental health may have had a bearing on his most serious miscalculation. In 1941 he decided to declare war on the USA, though he was still heavily involved on Russian, European and North African fronts.

Why he did so is a mystery. It was the war he most feared. However, his biographer, Joachim C. Fest pointed to some rationale for the move. Hitler, he said, had long since signed the Tripartite Pact with Japan and had pressed his Far Eastern allies to attack either the Soviet Union or British colonies in South-east Asia. Yet he had always stressed the undesirability of a war with America. When the Japanese attacked Pearl Harbour on 7 December 1941, Hitler was lost in admiration at the audacity of his Nipponese allies and, at their request, he declared war four days later.

His reasoning was that the Americans would be largely tied up in the Pacific and he could pursue his submarine war against Britain with greater ferocity by attacking American supply ships. It was also a chance to veil the crisis in Russia and, deep down, a recognition that his war plans had foundered.

Declaring war on the most powerful nation on earth had been yet another grand gesture. It was also a terrible blunder, the greater as he had already discovered the unreliability of his Italian allies, now spreading his war to Greece, Yugoslavia and soon back to Italy itself.

Field Marshal Carl Mannerheim with Hitler in Finland in 1942. The Führer was exhorting the Finnish commander to continue fighting the Russians with the aid of German reinforcements.

Der Führer als Tierfreund

A break from the war... Hitler feeds deer on a trip back to Bavaria and greets a veteran at his mountain retreat.

The Führer and the 'Desert Fox'... Field Marshal Irwin Rommel is warmly greeted by the man who would later order his death.

Isolationist America had never wanted to join in a European fight but, having been dragged in, all the energy of the New World was about to be poured into the struggle. Meanwhile, Britain's island fortress, protected by the Royal Navy and the RAF, could not be taken and was being supplied from the USA through the Lease Lend arrangement, by which President Roosevelt offered military aid to Britain. The submarine offensive was failing because Allied ships were better equipped to deal with them. In the air, the British tactic of blitzing the factories of the Ruhr had been boosted by the USA's entry into the war, with hugely intensified bombing raids. And in North Africa, Rommel, the 'Desert Fox', found his *Afrika Korps* bogged down through lack of reserves and supplies.

Hitler's response was indicative of his mental state. He began cutting himself off from his headquarters staff, became almost reclusive and increasingly reliant on drugs to keep him going. He was a man on the edge – and about to go over. When Rommel asked permission to retreat into the desert, he was told to fight on until victory or death. When General Paulus reported his stalled advance in Russia, he was ordered to move his headquarters into Stalingrad and throw up a defensive perimeter. Meanwhile, Hitler sent his troops into hitherto unoccupied areas of France.

This gaunt image appeared in the British press in February 1943 purporting to prove Hitler's failing health. It is obviously heavily retouched.

Field marshal Hermann Goering appears less than happy as he and Hitler discuss the progress of the war in 1943.

February 1943 and the war is not going well for Hitler as he uses a magnifying glass to trace the Eastern Front on a wall map.

The familiar scene in the Munich beer hall during Hitler's customary anniversary speech. But this is November 1943 and the mood is less than celebratory but predictably Goebbels and Goering applaud from the front row.

Not much joy in the faces of Hitler and Mussolini as they map out the progress of the war when they meet at the Reich government guesthouse near Salzburg in April 1943. Explaining the situation to them is General Kurt Zeitzler, chief of the army general staff.

Hitler on a Bavarian-bound plane back to the Berghof.

Albert Speer explains
progress in the
construction of the
'Atlantic Wall' to defend
the coastline against Allied
invasion.

The result was that on 2 November 1942 Lieutenant-General Bernard Montgomery finally dealt Rommel a crushing blow at El Alamein and Churchill was able to forecast: 'This is not the end. It is not even the beginning of the end. But it is, perhaps, the end of the beginning.' A week later Allied troops invaded Morocco and occupied the whole of French North Africa. Ten days later came the Russian counter-offensive at Stalingrad that led to General Paulus and 220,000 men being surrounded. By February 1943, the battle for Stalingrad was hopelessly lost and 91,000 German troops fell into Russian hands. Fewer than 10,000 were to return home, years later.

The inevitable result was that Hitler was driven ever closer to the verge of a breakdown. At the start of the Russian campaign, he had still been seen at the front and at mass rallies. When the defeats began, he lost the energy or the will to strike the familiar poses. His conversation deteriorated into monologue. He became even more irascible. In his fantasies, he adopted the role of a modern Macbeth, driven to his destiny by an overbearing fate, seeing himself as a giant going ever more flamboyantly to his doom in a blaze of glory. Instead of preparing for the worst he spent his time fantasising about world domination and taking morbid enjoyment from the vast arrays of enemy troops and firepower that were preparing their onslaught for him alone.

He became prey to melancholia, his left arm trembled permanently and he needed a cane to help him walk. It has been suggested that he suffered from Parkinson's disease, others blame venereal disease or the strychnine in the medicaments prescribed by Dr Morrell, who in civilian life had been a specialist in venereal diseases. By now the physician was dosing him with up to 28 different drugs a day. And as the doses became stronger, so too did the sedatives that were needed to calm his jangling nerves.

According to Norman Ohler, Morell made Hitler completely dependent on drugs, turning him into a virtual junkie. The author gained access to Morell's notes, which revealed that he gave him a total of 800 injections over a period of 1,349 days. Hitler became dependent on a drug called Eukodal, a pain killing narcotic with double the strength of conventional morphine. Ohler discovered that Hitler was first given the drug before a meeting with Mussolini in July 1943. At this point, with the opening of a second front in Sicily in July 1943, Italy was considering backing out of its alliance with Nazi Germany and, by capitulating, leaving his ally free to defend the line of the Alps. Hitler would have none of it and, after two Eukodal injections, felt so confident and forceful that he was able to convince Mussolini to stay with Germany for the time being. After the fall of 'Il Duce' on July 25, however, German forces were sent in to occupy the collapsing fascist state. Final defeat in Russia – at Moscow, Stalingrad and Kursk – left Hitler morosely pacing the 'Wolf's Lair', his HQ in East Prussia. He watched from there the long retreat in the east and in Italy. He waited for a miracle he knew would never come. He continued to think in continents and millennia, holding to his dream of an Aryan hierarchical superpower, with Slavic, oriental and black races enslaved and a world free of Jews. He was becoming unable to turn his mind to immediate practicalities.

By now, he had come to rely more and more on the support of Eva Braun – and of the drugs supplied by Dr Morrell. At the start of 1944, the German army was retreating back across the Ukraine and German cities were being bombed day and night. Yet Hitler was in a permanent reverie, being pumped with a cocktail of Eukodal, cocaine, vitamins, testosterone and animal hormones. The latter were to boost his libido, flagging by comparison with his lover, 22 years his junior. Since Eva was demanding similar potions, it is likely that their previously strained relationship was enjoying a false 'honeymoon period' at the Berghof, where mistress of the house Eva enjoyed extreme influence and where she largely controlled access to the Führer.

Even Dr Morrell was now becoming alarmed at the state of his VIP junkie patient. Hitler's hands would tremble uncontrollably and Morrell suspected that he was suffering from the early stages of Parkinson's Disease. An equal possibility is that the shaking was the effect of 'coming down' from his potent opiate cocktails.

It is unquestionable that the drugs were by now affecting Hitler's every decision. As defeat loomed, his plans for the New Order became more manic. The killing camps were put into overdrive. He sent out orders concerning the 'emigration' of entire races and the 'scrapping' of others. Like an old man, he harked back to the past: to Vienna, to the Great War, to his plans for a New Order. He had spies working in the ranks of his own armies. He was suspicious of anything new. He took little interest in jet engine development except to order that jets should be used only on bombers, not on fighters. Splitting the atom and the development of radar passed him by, unable to grasp their importance. Meanwhile, German cities were being reduced to rubble.

As he became ever more dependent on Morrell's drugs, his personal secretary, Martin Bormann, was allowed to take over the governance of the Reich — and, in effect, the war because he controlled every audience with Hitler.

Opposition within Germany was reaching epidemic proportions, with even Himmler planning to attempt a secret accord with the Allies. Yet Hitler seemed to bear a charmed life, adding to his feeling that he was a man of destiny. In the spring of 1943, two bombs planted in his plane failed to go off. A suicide bomb plot, organised for an occasion when Hitler would be examining new uniforms, failed because an allied air raid had destroyed the uniforms the day before. Another bomb went off prematurely and another suicide mission failed when the plotter was refused admittance to a conference.

The aftermath of the June 1940 assassination attempt at Hitler's headquarters in Rastenberg, East Prussia. The arrowed circle shows the spot where the bomb exploded.

Hitler returns to the scene with Italian leader Mussolini, who was by coincidence on a visit to the HQ at the time.

A wide-eyed Mussolini, appearing overjoyed at the Führer's lucky escape, returns to Italy to lead the fight against the advancing Allied forces.

Shortly after surviving the assassination plot, Hitler is photographed wearing an all-enveloping cloak – raising speculation that he was disguising an arm injury. The image, taken from a captured German newsreel, shows Himmler at his side and the face of Mussolini visible behind.

What a difference three months make. Hitler, relaxed with hand in pocket, is photographed in March 1944 – and again, looking gaunt, after the attempt on his life.

Hitler studying a map with Alfred Jodl, among his most loyal and longest serving generals, who was slightly injured in the July 1944 bomb plot.

Hitler aboard his private railway carriage. The somewhat partisan caption when this photograph was released in the West read: 'Uncertainty, indecision and worry are etched on his face'.

Hitler greets a worried ally: the Hungarian leader Franz Szalasy on a visit to Berlin in December 1944. In the background is Foreign Minister von Ribbentrop.

Nazi Germany faces defeat yet life goes on as normal at the Berghof. Military staff wait in the background as Hitler, seated between two ladies, entertains visitors to his mountain retreat.

Foregoing the normal Mercedes, Hitler takes a trip out from the Berghof in the latest Volkswagen – his own inspiration as, literally, the 'People's Car' that went on to become the most popular ever produced.

On 6 June 1944 the greatest armada ever assembled left the south coast of Britain to strike at Normandy in Northern France. As the Allies secured the beachheads and advanced on Caen and Paris, a long-time opponent of Hitler decided it was time to strike.

On 20 July, Colonel Count Claus Schenk von Stauffenberg, a 37-year-old crippled war hero of North Africa, possibly aided by his old C-in-C Rommel, now inspector of defences in Northern France, placed a bomb under a table at the Wolf's Lair. At the last minute, Hitler moved away from the table – and survived the explosion with only cuts and bruises. His revenge was terrible. Hundreds of suspects were rounded up, drummed out of the army and sentenced to death. The order was that they should be hanged ... as slowly as possible. Film of the hangings was presented to Hitler, who watched every last twitch with evident gratification. He further declared that all members of the plotters' families were equally guilty; children as young as three and uncles as old as 85 were arrested. Rommel himself was given the choice of suicide or death for all his family. He chose suicide. The executions continued until April 1945.

The Führer's bodyguard Bruno Gesche saw his master rapidly age before him. No longer invigorated with success, Hitler shuffled around his headquarters, directing his frustration not at the enemy but his own generals. It was they who had let down his great schemes. It was they who were conspiring against him — and he was right. Many generals wanted an end to the war while they could still negotiate a deal with the Western Allies.

The failed plot had one other effect on Hitler. Following discussions with Mussolini, now reinstalled as a puppet dictator, he placed Himmler in total command of army reserves and made Goebbels the 'Minister for Total War'. 'It takes a bomb under his backside to make Hitler see reason,' Goebbels noted in his diary.

Thus began the final effort. The organisational genius of the architect Albert Speer, promoted by Hitler to Minister of Armaments, saw to it that aircraft production was stepped up to its highest level of the war. Yet at the same time, Allied bombing of refineries and Russian advances across the Romanian oilfields denied the Luftwaffe the fuel to fly. Hitler's army was still nine million strong but was spread from Scandinavia to the Balkans. The advancing Red Army was encircling and capturing division after division to whom retreat had been denied.

Finland withdrew from the war in August, freeing more Russian troops for the German front, while British troops took Athens. Allied forces controlled Northern France as far as the Moselle. On September 11 an American patrol for the first time crossed into Germany. Although a Russian thrust into East Prussia was beaten back, the war had come home to the Fatherland.

At this period, Hitler's health deteriorated even further. He had retreated to his

Berlin bunker and never again left it, except once to visit the troops in the east, where his generals were shocked by his gaunt appearance. Soon he began complaining of constant headaches and nausea. In September he was laid low by a heart attack.

In this latter stage of the war, Hitler was left with two choices: to defend the long frontier to the east and fight off the ideological foe or to attack in the west. Typically, he chose to attack, in the apparent belief that the western allies would tire and join a common cause against Bolshevism. The Ardennes offensive, the so-called Battle of the Bulge, began on 16 December 1944 and was surprisingly successful for a time. Inevitably, however, it was thrown back through lack of supplies and overwhelming allied airpower.

A meeting with the Norwegian puppet premier Vidkun Quisling, whose name became a byword for collaboration and treason. Hitler had appointed him after invading his country but after Nazi Germany's defeat the legitimate Norwegian government had him executed by firing squad.

As the Red Army advances towards Berlin in March 1945, Hitler makes his last visit to his forces. Here he discusses the defence of the city with his staff at 9th Army HQ,

Among the most sickening photographs to emerge from the war... In late March 1945, with defeat inevitable, Hitler emerges from his bunker to encourage children to sacrifice themselves in the vain defence of the capital. Here he awards 12-year-old Hitler Youth soldier Alfred Czech the Iron Cross (second class) for his action against Russian forces.

By January 1945, the Russians were 100 miles from Berlin. On 30 January, Hitler delivered his last radio address to the German people. Victory would ultimately be theirs, he told them, through their unalterable will, their sacrifice and their abilities. On the same day, Speer sent a note to the Führer telling him the war was lost. Hitler prepared for an end in keeping with the grandiose Wagnerian operas that he loved. His fall would be so dramatic that he would become the stuff of myth and legend, and his desperate ideology would live on.

Children were recruited into the ranks for the last defence of the rubble of Berlin, as Hitler himself remained in his bunker beneath the Reich Chancellery. Yet there, too, he was no longer safe. For though his authority remained unchallenged until the final hours, even Speer, the man who had come closest to being a true friend, plotted to introduce poison gas into the ventilation system. By another amazing stroke of luck for the floundering Führer, the system was overhauled the day before the attempt and Hitler escaped yet again.

On 13 April, President Roosevelt died. For a time, Hitler was ecstatic. Three days later the Russians launched the final assault on Berlin. The capital was about to fall to the Soviet Army but Eva Braun now emerged from the Berghof to play out the final scene in their strange romance. On 7 March, despite Hitler's order not to come, she travelled by diplomatic car from Munich to Berlin and joined her lover in the *Führerbunker*.

The last time Hitler emerged above ground from the bunker was 20 April, his 56th birthday. All the top Nazis – Goering, Goebbels, Ribbentrop, Himmler, Bormann and Speer – met for the last time and urged the abandonment of Berlin and a last stand at the Berghof in Bavaria. Hitler chose instead to die among the ruins, though he allowed Goering to flee south before the capital was encircled.

The Soviets surrounding Berlin, under Marshal Zhukov, had 20 armies, 2.5 million soldiers and 40,000 field guns, mortars and rocket launchers. The exhausted German armies were incapable of holding them back. With total annihilation inevitable, Hitler spurned his generals' entreaties, repeatedly ordering: 'Hold the line or perish.'

April 22 was the watershed for Hitler. The afternoon conference he had called finally convinced him that Armageddon was inevitable – and it became clear that the founder of the 'Thousand Year Reich', having been denied world domination, now wanted his epitaph to be an apocalyptic defeat. He ranted and raved at the failings of his armies and the disloyalty of their generals, then said: 'The war is lost. Do whatever you like. I am not giving any more orders.' The ruins of the capital would now be defended by a few *Volkssturm* battalions, consisting of old men and 4,000 teenagers of the Hitler Youth.

Some among the hierarchy took matters into their own hands. Hitler's protégé Speer disobeyed a direct order to raze Germany's infrastructure to the ground.

From southern Germany, Goering telegraphed the bunker seeking authority to assume the role of Führer if the worst should befall. Hitler's response was to accuse him of high treason. Another black day for the Führer was 28 April, with news that Italian partisans had shot Mussolini and his mistress Clara Petacci. Shortly afterwards another unwelcome message arrived: a report that Himmler had tried to negotiate surrender terms with the Western powers. According to a witness, the apoplectic Hitler 'turned a dark red and his face became almost unrecognisable'. Unable to take revenge against the SS leader, he ordered the arrest of his representative at HQ, Hermann Fegelein, and had him shot – extraordinary vengeance, since the functionary was married to Eva Braun's pregnant sister.

Eva could not save her brother-in-law but she had a greater destiny in prospect. Her lover had at last agreed to make her his wife. At one o'clock in the morning of 29 April, Adolf Hitler and Eva Braun emerged from their private quarters, her arm through his. Goebbels and Bormann were witnesses as local magistrate Walter Wagner, brought in to carry out a civil service of marriage, nervously asked the bride and groom to confirm that they were of 'pure Aryan descent and free of hereditary diseases'. Rings, believed to have been taken from the bodies of Gestapo prisoners, were exchanged and Wagner declared: 'This marriage is legal before the law'. After the ceremony, the couple returned to their private rooms for tea and sandwiches with senior staff. The strictly teetotal groom accepted a small glass of wine. Eva quaffed champagne. They then retired, seemingly to their separate bedrooms.

When his valet Heinz Linge knocked on Hitler's door at 11am, he found him lying on his bed fully dressed. Three hours later he sat down for a light lunch with Eva and some of his remaining private staff, including his ever-loyal secretary Traudl Junge. Overnight she had finished typing her master's dictated last will and testament. Even this was largely a polemic against the Jews, though on a personal note he donated his paintings to the town of Linz. Bormann was named his executor, Admiral von Doenitz as his successor and Goebbels as head of the government.

They turned out to be less than long-term appointments. For as Hitler planned his last hours on earth, a not much better fate awaited many of those who had so enthusiastically chosen to follow his route to oblivion...

Joseph Goebbels made his own preparations to commit suicide in the bunker, which he did on May 1 after first poisoning his six children and shooting his wife. Heinrich Himmler, having failed to make a peace deal with the Allies, was captured by the British on May 21 but bit on a cyanide capsule before he could face trial as a war criminal. The following year, Hermann Goering similarly committed suicide two hours before his scheduled execution at Nuremberg. Foreign Minister Joachim von Ribbentrop was hanged at Nuremberg. So was party propagandist and editor Julius Streicher and Nazi philosopher Alfred Rosenberg. Rudolph Hess,

Grinning in the face of defeat... This photograph was taken outside Hitler's private quarters within the Führerbunker in April 1945. In the centre is one of his SS bodyguards and his naval attaché. On the left is the sinister Dr Morrell.

A Russian soldier tries the telephone in Eva Braun's modest bedroom. The box on her bedside table contains phials of poison.

After Germany's capitulation, American soldiers searched Hitler's bunker. In the Führer's conference room, a sergeant illuminates the wreckage while holding a ring of keys to the private apartments.

A US soldier looks through drawers in Eva Braun's bedroom.

Americans search by candlelight for clues to the dictator's last days.

Another American in the Führer's own modest bedroom.

Snapshot of history... In the garden exit of the Führerbunker, an American soldier takes a souvenir photograph of two comrades examining the spot on which they believe the bodies of Hitler and Eva Braun were burned.

Last remnants of the reich... An East German demolition team blow up the remains of Hitler's bunker in June 1947.

sentenced to life imprisonment, was found hanged in Berlin's Spandau Jail in 1987. Albert Speer fared slightly better; sentenced to 20 years imprisonment at Nuremberg, he was freed in 1966 and died 15 years later on a visit to Britain. Martin Bormann's fate is less certain. Recent DNA evidence from a skull dug up in Berlin supports reports that he was killed while trying to escape Berlin on May 2, 1945 – although theories still abound that he escaped to South America by U-boat.

As for Hitler himself, on 30 April 1945, the morning after his marriage, with death and destruction all around him, and with the rats scurrying from the cellar or taking their poison, it was their leader's turn to face the inevitable. Cyanide and a bullet would succeed where more than 40 attempts on his life had failed. He had already ordered the poison to be tested on his beloved German shepherd Blondi, a handler having crushed a capsule in her mouth with a pair of pliers. Blondi dropped 'as if struck by lightning'. Her puppies, born in the bunker, were also disposed of. Hitler inspected Blondi's body to satisfy himself that cyanide worked as swiftly as he had been told.

At about 3pm Hitler said farewell to his valet and told Linge: 'You know what you must do. Ensure my body is burned and my possessions destroyed.' He walked into his study, where Eva was waiting, and closed the door. At 3.30 there was a brief lull in the barrage of enemy artillery fire – and a single shot rang out. Heinz Linge waited briefly then opened the door and was followed inside by Martin Bormann. They were greeted with the sight of Hitler and his bride slumped on the sofa. He had shot himself in the right temple and his head was leaning back towards the blood-spattered wall. She had bitten on a cyanide phial that she had kept in a small brass box that lay open on the low table in front of them. Her legs were drawn towards her and her face was contorted. Two revolvers lay on the floor, one used by Hitler and the other kept as a back-up.

Linge, along with Hitler's adjutant Otto Gunsche and his long-time chauffeur-bodyguard Erich Kempka, helped wrap their leader's body in a blanket and carry it up to the Reich Chancellery garden. When Bormann tried to hoist Eva's corpse out of the bunker, Kempka took the body from him and insisted on bearing it up himself, remarking that Bormann was carrying her 'like a sack of potatoes'. The bodies were tipped into a shallow grave. Linge, Gunsche and Kempka poured petrol over them. Goebbels joined them, thoughtfully producing a box of matches. A lighted piece of paper was thrown onto the funeral pyre and, as the bodies burned, the Führer received his last tribute as his remaining bodyguards raised their arms in a final Nazi salute.

Back inside the bunker, most of the soldiers and secretaries were getting drunk on schnapps. Russians entered the Reich Chancellery the following day. That morning, Hamburg radio announced: 'The Führer has fallen at his command post fighting to the last breath against Bolshevism and for Germany.' In Moscow, Josef Stalin commented: 'So that's the end of the bastard.' In July Winston Churchill visited the site where Hitler's body was burned and said: 'This is what would have happened to us if they had won the war.' Then he gave a 'V' for Victory sign. The nightmare was over.

Principal Dates

1889	Adolf Hitler born.
1903	Death of father, Alois.
1905	Move to Vienna.
1907	Death of mother, Klara.
1913	Move to Munich.
1914	Arrest for draft-dodging; later declared unfit for military service. World War I starts. Joins Bavarian regiment. Action at Ypres. Awarded Iron Cross (Second Class).
1918	Awarded Iron Cross (First Class). Abdication of Kaiser Wilhelm II following naval mutiny at Kiel and unrest in Germany. Defeat of Germany; Armistice signed.
1919	Germany signs Treaty of Versailles.
1919	Joins German Workers' Party.
1923	Beer Hall Putsch. Nazi party banned. Writes Mein Kampf in jail.
1925	Re-formation of the Nazi party.
1926	Germany joins League of Nations.
1927	First Nuremberg rally.
1928	Nazis win 12 seats in Reichstag.
1929	Wall Street Crash: worldwide recession.
1930	Nazis win 107 Reichstag seats with 6.4 million votes.
1931	Stands against Hindenburg as President and secures 30.1% of vote.
1932	Hitler becomes a German citizen.
1933	Becomes Reich Chancellor. Reichstag fire is followed by suspension of civil rights. Enabling Law grants Hitler dictatorial powers for four years. Mass boycott of Jewish shops and services begins. Trades unions and all political parties except Nazis banned. Hitler signs concordat with Vatican. Burning of books (other than those approved by the party) begins. Germany leaves League of Nations.
1934	Night of the Long Knives. Death of President von Hindenburg. Hitler declared Führer. Army takes personal oath to Hitler.
1935	Conscription introduced. Nuremberg Laws, declaring Jews second-class citizens.
1936	German Condor Legion fights in Spanish Civil War. Reoccupation of demilitarised Rhineland. Berlin Olympic Games, where Negro Jesse Owens shatters Aryan myth by winning four gold medals.

1937	Anti-Comintern Pact signed with Italy. First autobahn built.
1938	German troops occupy demilitarised Rhineland. *Anschluss* of Austria. Munich agreement with Chamberlain leads to invasion of Sudetenland. *Krystallnacht*: pogrom against German Jews begins.
1939	Czechoslovakia crisis. Munich conference. Occupation of Czechoslovakia. Occupation of Bohemia and Moravia. Nazi-Soviet pact signed. Invasion of Poland. Start of World War II.
1940	Invasion of Denmark, Norway, Holland, Belgium, France and Luxembourg. Evacuation of British Expeditionary Force from Dunkirk. France signs armistice with Germany. Battle of Britain.
1941	Operation Barbarossa: invasion of Russia. Final Solution (genocide of the Jews) agreed. War with America after Japanese attack on Pearl Harbour.
1942	Adolf Eichmann takes over administration of Final Solution. Battle of El Alamein. Defeat in North Africa.
1943	German defeats at Stalingrad, Moscow, Kursk. Retreat from Russia. Fall of Mussolini. Allied invasion of Italy. Italy surrenders.
1944	July Plot: Hitler survives bomb in his HQ.
1945	War in Germany. Suicide of Hitler and Eva Braun. German surrender.